GREAT PRO SPORTS CHAMPIONSHIPS

GREAT MLB WORLD SERIES CHAMPIONSHIPS

by Ethan Olson

BrightPoint Press

San Diego, CA

© 2024 BrightPoint Press
an imprint of ReferencePoint Press, Inc.
Printed in the United States

For more information, contact:
BrightPoint Press
PO Box 27779
San Diego, CA 92198
www.BrightPointPress.com

ALL RIGHTS RESERVED.

No part of this work covered by the copyright hereon may be reproduced or used in any form or by any means—graphic, electronic, or mechanical, including photocopying, recording, taping, web distribution, or information storage retrieval systems—without the written permission of the publisher.

LIBRARY OF CONGRESS CATALOGING-IN-PUBLICATION DATA

Names: Olson, Ethan, author.
Title: Great MLB World Series championships / by Ethan Olson.
Description: San Diego, CA: BrightPoint Press, [2024] | Series: Great pro sports championships | Includes bibliographical references and index. | Audience: Ages 13 | Audience: Grades 7-9
Identifiers: LCCN 2023004149 (print) | LCCN 2023004150 (eBook) | ISBN 9781678206543 (hardcover) | ISBN 9781678206550 (eBook)
Subjects: LCSH: World Series (Baseball)--History--Juvenile literature.
Classification: LCC GV878.4 .O55 2024 (print) | LCC GV878.4 (eBook) | DDC 796.357/646--dc23/eng/20230213
LC record available at https://lccn.loc.gov/2023004149
LC eBook record available at https://lccn.loc.gov/2023004150

CONTENTS

AT A GLANCE	4
INTRODUCTION A GREAT AMERICAN TRADITION	6
CHAPTER ONE "AIN'T THIS FUN?"	10
CHAPTER TWO WORST TO FIRST	22
CHAPTER THREE THE DYNASTY ENDS	34
CHAPTER FOUR THE LONG WAIT	46
Glossary	58
Source Notes	59
For Further Research	60
Index	62
Image Credits	63
About the Author	64

AT A GLANCE

- The World Series was first played in 1903. Since then, it has taken place at the end of every Major League Baseball (MLB) season except for 1904 and 1994.

- The 1975 champion Cincinnati Reds featured one of the greatest lineups baseball has ever seen. But the "Big Red Machine" was pushed to the limit in the World Series by the Boston Red Sox in a series that featured one of the most famous home runs ever witnessed in the sport.

- The record-setting 1991 World Series featured five one-run games, four walk-off victories, and three games decided in extra innings. In the end, the Minnesota Twins outlasted the Atlanta Braves.

- In 2001, circumstances beyond baseball meant the World Series extended into November for the first time in MLB history as the Arizona Diamondbacks defeated the New York Yankees.

- By 2016, Chicago Cubs fans had endured 108 years of pain without their team winning the World Series. The Cubs squared off against a Cleveland team that had not won it all since 1948.

- The seventh game of the 2016 World Series was made even more dramatic by a timely visit from Mother Nature. As the game went into the tenth inning, a rain delay made both sets of nervous fans wait just a little longer for the thrilling finish. When it was all over, so was the Cubs fans' wait for a title.

INTRODUCTION

A GREAT AMERICAN TRADITION

Game 7 of the 2016 World Series between the Chicago Cubs and Cleveland Indians was tied 6–6 heading into the tenth inning. Both sets of fans were on edge. Neither team had won a World Series in over half a century. But soon one of those **droughts** would end. Suddenly, play was brought to a halt. A flash rainstorm had rolled into Cleveland, Ohio.

The teams retreated to their **clubhouses** and waited. Finally, after seventeen minutes, the game was ready to resume. The Cubs were up to bat, and they came out swinging. Kyle Schwarber singled to right

Nervous fans from both Chicago and Cleveland watched Game 7 of the 2016 World Series.

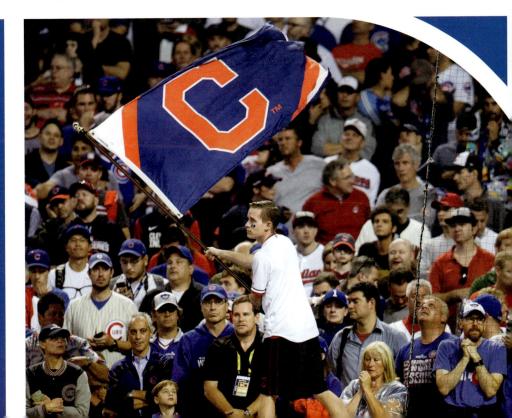

to start the inning. He was quickly replaced by a speedier runner, Albert Almora Jr. Cleveland pitcher Bryan Shaw retired Kris Bryant. After an intentional walk of Cubs first baseman Anthony Rizzo, Ben Zobrist swatted a double to left field. Almora scored to break the tie. It was a clutch hit by Zobrist on baseball's biggest stage.

THE FALL CLASSIC

Moments like Zobrist's base hit have made the World Series special for more than one hundred years. The World Series is one of America's greatest sports traditions.

Chicago's Ben Zobrist (right) was named Most Valuable Player (MVP) of the 2016 World Series.

Since 1903, the championship's drama has played out in October and November. Heroes of the World Series have included baseball legends as well as less well-known players. Some moments have lasted in fans' memories for years after they happened.

1

"AIN'T THIS FUN?"

One long streak had to end in the 1975 World Series. The Cincinnati Reds had not won a championship since 1940. The Boston Red Sox had not captured a World Series title since 1918.

Manager Sparky Anderson led a Reds team with one of the most fearsome lineups in Major League Baseball (MLB). In 1975, the "Big Red Machine" scored 840 runs. That was the highest total in MLB. In doing so, the Reds won an MLB-best 108 games.

Second baseman Joe Morgan was one of the many stars that made up the Cincinnati Reds' powerful lineup in 1975.

The Red Sox had won 95 times during the regular season. Boston had also just beaten the Oakland Athletics in the American League Championship Series (ALCS). The A's were the three-time defending champions.

MVPs

The teams in the 1975 series featured the Most Valuable Players (MVPs) of each league. Cincinnati second baseman Joe Morgan won the award in the National League (NL). The American League (AL) winner was Boston rookie center fielder Fred Lynn. He also won the Rookie of the Year Award. At the time, Lynn was the only major leaguer ever to take both honors in the same season.

To the surprise of many, the Red Sox shut down the Reds in Game 1. Starter Luis Tiant pitched a 6–0 shutout at Fenway Park in Boston, Massachusetts. Boston then took a 2–1 lead into the ninth inning of Game 2. But Ken Griffey's run-scoring double with two outs knocked home the winning run in Cincinnati's 3–2 win.

INTERFERENCE

The Reds stormed out to a 5–1 lead in Game 3 before Boston fought back. Dwight Evans tied the game 5–5 with a two-run homer with one out in the ninth. That set the stage for the most controversial moment of the series. In the bottom of the tenth inning, Cincinnati's César Gerónimo led off with a single. Pinch hitter Ed Armbrister tried to bunt Gerónimo over to second. When Boston catcher Carlton Fisk came out to play the ball, he appeared to bump into Armbrister. Fisk's throw to second base sailed into center field. Gerónimo took third on the **error**.

The Red Sox argued that Armbrister had interfered with Fisk. If so, Armbrister should have been out, and Gerónimo would be sent back to first base. But the umpires

Boston catcher Carlton Fisk (27) collides with Cincinnati's Ed Armbrister during the tenth inning of Game 3.

didn't change the call. Boston was still angry three batters later when Cincinnati's Joe Morgan singled home Gerónimo to win the game.

Boston shook off that disappointment in Game 4 to win 5–4. But Cincinnati routed Boston 6–2 in Game 5. The teams were headed back to Boston, and the Reds had a chance to win it all.

STAY FAIR

The sixth game of the 1975 World Series is widely considered to be one of the best games in baseball history. But it took a while to get started. The game was delayed three days by rain.

This time Boston jumped out early. Center fielder Fred Lynn hit a three-run homer in the bottom of the first inning. But the Reds stormed back for six unanswered runs.

A Fenway Park stadium worker clears water off the field after heavy rain delayed Game 6 of the 1975 World Series.

Boston was in deep trouble heading into the bottom of the eighth down 6–3. Lynn and third baseman Rico Petrocelli both reached base. Anderson brought reliever Rawly Eastwick out of the **bullpen** to try to stop the **rally**. Eastwick got the next two batters. He then faced pinch hitter Bernie Carbo.

A former Red, Carbo was struggling against the hard-throwing Eastwick. After barely fouling off one 2–2 pitch, Carbo drilled a long fly ball to center field. It settled in the seats to tie the game. The crowd at Fenway Park exploded with joy.

Rounding the bases, Carbo passed Reds third baseman Pete Rose. "Don't you wish you were this strong?" Carbo chirped at his old teammate.

Rose replied, "Ain't this fun?"[1]

Despite great chances to score on both sides, the game stayed 6–6 heading into the twelfth inning. Fisk led off the

Fisk watches his game-winning home run in Game 6.

bottom half. Fisk was a New Hampshire native. He had been a lifelong fan of the Red Sox. On the second pitch of the inning, he sent a long fly ball down the left field line. It had the distance, but no one knew if it would stay fair. Fisk danced up the first base line, waving his arms to will the ball where he wanted it. It eventually struck the foul pole for a home run. As Fisk rounded the bases, fans poured onto the field.

Boston took an early 3–0 lead in Game 7 the next night. A home run by Cincinnati's Tony Pérez cut it to 3–2 in the sixth. Then Rose tied it with a run-scoring single in the seventh. Morgan drove in the winning run on a single in the ninth. Longtime Boston star Carl Yastrzemski flew out to end the game. The Reds were World Series champions. Their drought was over, but Boston's lived on. The Red Sox would not win a championship until 2004.

Cincinnati fans who were in Boston for Game 7 flooded the field and surrounded the team after the Reds won.

Despite the Reds' victory, the lasting play of the World Series was Fisk's home run. It remains one of the most talked about moments in baseball history.

2

WORST TO FIRST

In 1990, the Atlanta Braves were the worst team in baseball. The Minnesota Twins weren't much better. They finished last in the AL West. No team in baseball history had ever gone from last place in their league to the World Series the next year. But in 1991, both teams did it.

Whichever group won the series would be a true Cinderella champion.

The series opened at the Hubert H. Humphrey Metrodome in Minneapolis,

Twins third baseman Scott Leius high-fives the team bat boy after hitting a tiebreaking home run in the bottom of the eighth inning of Game 2.

Minnesota. After Twins pitcher Jack Morris led the way in a 5–2 win in Game 1, the next three games were all nail-biters. All three were decided by one run. The Twins won the second game 3–2 on a home run in the eighth inning by rookie third baseman Scott Leius.

In Atlanta, Georgia, the Braves won Game 3 in twelve innings. Atlanta then won Game 4 in the ninth on a **walk-off** sacrifice fly by third-string catcher Jerry Willard. The Braves completed the southern sweep with a 14–5 blowout win in Game 5. The teams moved back to Minnesota with Atlanta one

Atlanta's Mark Lemke slides past Minnesota catcher Brian Harper to score the winning run in Game 3.

win away from a championship. The Twins needed a big boost to get back into the series. Fortunately, one of Minnesota's stars was ready to step up.

KIRBY'S MOMENT

Twins center fielder Kirby Puckett hit just 3-for-18 through the first five games. But Puckett knocked home a run with a triple in the first inning of Game 6 as part of a two-run Twins rally. In the third inning he made a leaping catch against the wall in left-center field. Puckett drove in another run in the fifth.

Minnesota still couldn't shake the Braves. Atlanta eventually tied the game 3–3. It stayed that way into the bottom of the eleventh inning. Puckett was leading off for Minnesota. As he warmed up, he

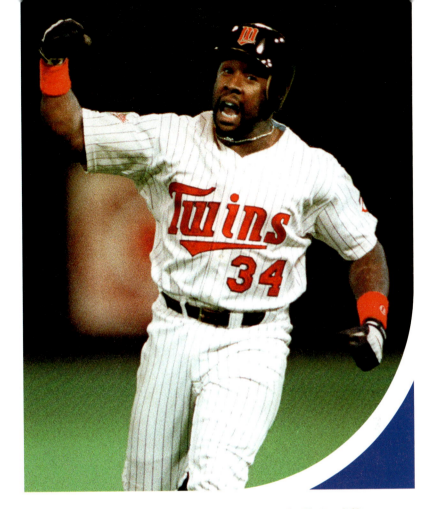

Minnesota's Kirby Puckett pumps his fist while rounding the bases after hitting his game-winning home run in Game 6.

looked at teammate Chili Davis and said he was going to bunt to get on base. That way, Davis could drive him in. Davis had a different plan.

"You get a good hanging changeup, hit it out," Davis replied. "Let's go home."[2]

The Twins' star listened. On a 2–1 pitch, Puckett smacked a walk-off home run to left-center field. He pumped his fist as he rounded the bases. The hit capped off one of the greatest individual games in World Series history. It also kept the Twins alive.

THE SHOWDOWN

The story of Game 7 was the starting pitchers. The Twins' starter was the **veteran** Morris. The native Minnesotan had spent many years with the Detroit Tigers.

Jack Morris threw 126 pitches for the Twins during his ten-inning shutout in Game 7.

In 1991, he had come home to sign with the Twins. Atlanta's twenty-four-year-old righty John Smoltz had grown up in Michigan. Morris had been Smoltz's favorite player.

Now the two locked horns in an epic pitcher's duel.

The game remained scoreless into the eighth inning. Then Morris loaded the bases with only one out. The next batter was Braves first baseman Sid Bream. He bounced a ball to Kent Hrbek at first. Hrbek fired home to get one out. Catcher Brian Harper threw back to first. He retired Bream for an unlikely inning-ending double play.

The Twins also loaded the bases with one out in the bottom half. During the rally, Braves manager Bobby Cox removed

Smoltz from the game. Lefty Mike Stanton came on and faced Hrbek, another native Minnesotan. The Twins slugger hit a soft line drive right at second baseman Mark Lemke. Lemke stepped on the bag to double off a runner and end the inning.

Morris kept the Braves scoreless through the top of the tenth. It was now up to the Twins' offense to make him a winner.

FULL CIRCLE

The 1991 World Series was the first to end on an extra-inning Game 7 since 1924. The winners that year were the Washington Senators. In 1961 the Senators moved to Minnesota and became the Twins.

Left fielder Dan Gladden led off the bottom half with a bloop double. A sacrifice bunt and two intentional walks loaded the bases for pinch hitter Gene Larkin. There was only one out. Cox had to bring the outfield in to try to get Gladden at the plate on a short fly ball. But Larkin bashed reliever Alejandro Peña's first pitch to deep left. It dropped in for a long single. Gladden trotted home, where he was greeted first by Morris, then the rest of the team.

Morris won the World Series MVP Award. He had won two games in the series for his hometown team. And his ten-inning

Minnesota's Dan Gladden leaps in the air before heading home for the winning run in Game 7.

shutout in Game 7 still ranks as one of the most amazing World Series pitching performances ever. "Somebody had to go home a loser. But nobody was a loser in my mind," Morris said later.[3]

3
THE DYNASTY ENDS

Entering the 2001 season, the New York Yankees had won three straight World Series. Many around baseball felt the team was unbeatable. They had superstars all over the field. **Ace** pitcher Roger Clemens won his sixth career Cy Young

Award. Closer Mariano Rivera was nearly impossible to hit.

However, the Arizona Diamondbacks were not afraid. Arizona had only come into existence in 1998 as an expansion team.

Manager Joe Torre (dark jacket) led the New York Yankees to World Series wins in 1996, 1998, 1999, and 2000.

But in a short time, the team had become a contender full of veteran stars. The two biggest were starting pitchers Curt Schilling and Randy Johnson. Schilling was a confident, hard thrower. But no one threw harder than Johnson. The snarling 6 foot, 10 inch lefty terrified batters.

On September 11, 2001, terrorist attacks shocked the United States. Baseball shut down for several days while the country recovered. The World Series would extend into November for the first time.

In New York, the twin towers of the World Trade Center both collapsed in the attack.

Feelings of shock and loss spread throughout the city.

When games resumed, fans in New York rallied around the Yankees. Even people who normally hated the dominant team pulled for New York this time. But Schilling and Johnson dominated the

HONORING THE FALLEN

The attack on the World Trade Center in New York City collapsed two 110-story skyscrapers and killed 2,753 people. One of the items that was recovered from the wreckage was an American flag that had flown above one of the towers. The tattered flag was raised at Yankee Stadium during the World Series as a tribute.

first two games. Both were lopsided home victories for the Diamondbacks.

NOVEMBER BASEBALL

The Yankees scratched back a win in Game 3. Game 4 began on Halloween night. And New York fans' worst fears played out when Arizona took a 3–1 lead in the top of the eighth. To close the game out in the ninth, Arizona brought on righty Byung-Hyun Kim. New York's Tino Martinez responded with a two-out, two-run shot to right-center field to tie the game. Yankee Stadium went wild.

In his career, Yankees closer Mariano Rivera pitched ninety-six postseason innings and allowed only eleven earned runs.

Star shortstop Derek Jeter came up to bat with two outs in the bottom of the tenth inning. After he took the first pitch, the clock struck midnight. On Kim's 3–2 pitch, Jeter sliced a long fly ball to right that barely cleared the fence for a home run. The first MLB run ever scored in November evened the series.

The Diamondbacks took a 2–0 lead into the bottom of the ninth of Game 5. Arizona manager Bob Brenly went back to Kim to close the game. After a leadoff double, Kim got the next two outs. New York third baseman Scott Brosius then corked a

After his walk-off home run in Game 3, the Yankees' Derek Jeter was given the nickname "Mr. November."

two-run homer to left. Kim nearly collapsed on the mound after losing a second consecutive lead. He was immediately removed from the game. The Yankees won on a walk-off single in the twelfth inning.

Brenly turned to Johnson in Game 6. The lefty struck out seven over seven innings while Arizona's offense piled up a 15–2 victory.

THE BLOOPER

Game 7 featured a pitching matchup for the ages. Schilling started for Arizona. Clemens was on the mound for New York. The two aces didn't disappoint. The game was scoreless until the Diamondbacks scored in the bottom of the sixth. Martinez tied the game the next inning on a one-out single.

In the eighth, New York second baseman Alfonso Soriano hit a long solo home run to left field. Schilling didn't finish the inning.

Curt Schilling (left) and Randy Johnson (right) had a combined record of 43–12 for the Diamondbacks in 2001.

Brenly eventually surprised everyone by bringing Johnson out of the bullpen. The gamble worked. Johnson held the Yankees scoreless through the ninth.

Down 2–1, the Diamondbacks still had to score against Rivera in the bottom half.

The intimidating closer had allowed only six earned runs in 78 2/3 postseason innings.

Arizona put two runners on with one out. Then shortstop Tony Womack doubled to tie the game. Rivera hit the next batter to load the bases. That brought up Arizona star Luis Gonzalez. The left fielder had led the team that year with 57 home runs. But on an 0–1 pitch, all he managed was a soft line drive toward shortstop. Jeter was playing shallow, and the ball looped over his head for a hit. Jay Bell scored, and the Diamondbacks were champions for the first time ever.

Luis Gonzalez (left) celebrates his World Series–winning walk-off hit with Arizona first-base coach Eddy Rodriguez.

After the game, Gonzalez said, "That's what everybody dreams about. I can't believe it's me in that situation."[4] Few could believe what the Diamondbacks had done. It was an incredible end to a memorable series.

4
THE LONG WAIT

By 2016, several generations of Chicago Cubs fans had come and gone without seeing the team win a championship. The last Cubs World Series win had come 108 years earlier, in 1908. The Cubs hadn't even played in the World Series since 1945. Many fans thought the team was cursed.

But the team was still incredibly popular both in and outside of Chicago. Over the years, they had picked up the nickname "Lovable Losers."

Cleveland fans didn't feel much better. The team had failed to win the World Series

Cubs fans file into Wrigley Field for Game 3, the first World Series game played at the ballpark since 1945.

since 1948. In that time, Cleveland had only reached the Fall Classic three times.

Against that backdrop, the two teams met in the 2016 World Series. Even the players were wrapped up in the history. Before the games started, Cleveland first baseman Mike Napoli spoke to the *New York Times.* "The baseball gods are really happy right now," Napoli said. "I think it's going to be a special World Series."[5]

The Cubs had been the best pitching team in baseball that year. But Cleveland ace Corey Kluber's dominant start stole the show in Game 1. He struck out eight

Corey Kluber won eighteen games for Cleveland during the 2016 season, and four more in the playoffs.

batters in the first three innings on the way to a 6–0 home win.

Chicago answered in Game 2 with a 5–1 victory. But Cleveland took the next two games in Chicago as the Cubs were held to only two total runs. Cleveland had a commanding 3–1 lead in the series. But no one in Ohio was ready to celebrate. As team manager Terry Francona said after the game, "We have a ways to go."[6]

THE COMEBACK

The Cubs, of course, had even further to go. But they started to crawl back with a 3–2 win in Game 5. The second one-run game of the series pushed the games back to Cleveland.

Chicago's offense finally got rolling in Game 6, led by the team's stars. Third baseman Kris Bryant and first

From left, Cubs players Anthony Rizzo, Addison Russell, Ben Zobrist, and Kyle Schwarber celebrate Russell's Game 6 grand slam.

baseman Anthony Rizzo both homered.

Shortstop Addison Russell hit the first World Series grand slam in eleven years. The Cubs blasted Cleveland 9–3.

That set the stage for the historic seventh game. Chicago outfielder Dexter Fowler made even more history in the game's first at bat. He became the first player to ever lead off a World Series seventh game with a home run.

The Cubs built a 6–3 lead heading into the bottom of the eighth. But after a two-out single, Chicago manager Joe Maddon went to his bullpen. He had one of the nastiest relievers in the league ready to go. Lefty Aroldis Chapman routinely threw over 100 miles per hour (161 kmh). Chicago fans hoped he could shut down the game.

Cleveland's Rajai Davis watches his two-run game-tying home run leave the ballpark in the eighth inning of Game 7.

Cleveland had other ideas. Outfielder Brandon Guyer doubled to bring in a run. The next batter was Rajai Davis. On a 2–2 pitch, Davis connected with a low fastball. He hit a line drive that just cleared the fence in left. The game was tied.

The Cubs put a runner on in the ninth but failed to score. Chapman cruised through the bottom half. Extra innings would be needed for the first time in the series. But then the rain came, delaying play for nearly twenty minutes. As the teams moved to the clubhouse to escape the weather, Chicago outfielder Jason Heyward sensed his Cubs needed a boost. He told the group, "We're the best team in baseball. Stick together and we're going to win this game."[7]

The Cubs did just that, scoring two runs in the top half of the tenth inning. Cubs fans around the country wondered if this was

Cubs outfielder Jayson Heyward's speech during the rain delay in Game 7 pumped up the team before the tenth inning.

the moment the long streak would finally end. Many who traveled to Cleveland's Progressive Field held their breath.

However, the drama wasn't over. Cubs reliever Carl Edwards Jr. got two quick outs in the bottom of the tenth. Then he

EXTRA-INNING GAME 7s IN WORLD SERIES HISTORY

1912: Boston Red Sox 3, New York Giants 2 (10 innings)*

1924: Washington Senators 4, New York Giants 3 (12 innings)

1991: Minnesota Twins 1, Atlanta Braves 0 (10 innings)

1997: Florida Marlins 3, Cleveland Indians 2 (11 innings)

2016: Chicago Cubs 8, Cleveland Indians 7 (10 innings)

*Game 8 of the series, due to one earlier game ending in a tie.

The 2016 World Series featured one of the longest Game 7s in history.

walked Guyer. Two pitches later, with Guyer on second, Davis struck again, knocking in a run with a single to make it 8–7. Maddon went to lefty Mike Montgomery to try to get the last out.

Cleveland's Michael Martinez was up next. He bounced an 0–1 pitch to third base. Bryant charged it and fired to first. Rizzo caught the final out, then stuffed the historic ball in his back pocket before joining the celebration. Fans on Chicago's north side could finally celebrate. After 108 years and one of the longest Game 7s in baseball history, the Cubs were champions at last.

THE CELEBRATION

A crowd of nearly 5 million people turned up for the Cubs' victory parade in downtown Chicago. In addition, the Chicago River was dyed blue for the event.

GLOSSARY

ace

The best starting pitcher on a team.

bullpen

The area on a baseball field set aside for relief pitchers to warm up.

clubhouses

Another term for locker rooms, the places at the ballpark where players get ready for a game.

droughts

Long periods without success.

error

When a baseball fielder misplays a ball.

rally

An inning in which a team scores several runs.

veteran

Someone who has played a professional sport for many seasons.

walk-off

Won by the home team in its final at-bat.

SOURCE NOTES

CHAPTER ONE: "AIN'T THIS FUN?"

1. Quoted in Al Doyle, "The Game I'll Never Forget," *Baseball Digest,* November 2005. www.baseball-reference.com.

CHAPTER TWO: WORST TO FIRST

2. Quoted in *Magic in Minnesota: Remembering the 1991 World Series Championship.* Directed by Major League Baseball, A&E Home Video, 2011.

3. Quoted in Tim Wendell, *Down to the Last Pitch: How the 1991 Minnesota Twins and Atlanta Braves Gave Us the Best World Series of All Time.* Boston, MA: Da Capo Press, 2014, p. 193.

CHAPTER THREE: THE DYNASTY ENDS

4. Quoted in Jim McLennan, "Ten Years On: Diamondbacks 3, Yankees 2—Never Say Die-mondbacks Swipe New York's Champagne," *AZ Snake Pit*, November 5, 2011. www.azsnakepit.com.

CHAPTER FOUR: THE LONG WAIT

5. Quoted in Tyler Kepner, "World Series Preview: For Cubs or Indians, Decades of Waiting Are Nearly Over," *New York Times,* October 24, 2016. www.nytimes.com.

6. Quoted in "Corey Kluber Helps Indians by Cubs, to 3–1 World Series Lead," *ESPN*, October 30, 2016. www.espn.com.

7. Quoted in Tom Verducci, "Book Excerpt: Go Behind the Scenes of the Cubs' World Series Game 7 Win," *Sports Illustrated*, March 14, 2017. www.si.com.

FOR FURTHER RESEARCH

BOOKS

John Allen, *The Science and Technology of Baseball*. San Diego, CA: ReferencePoint Press, 2020.

Shirley Duke, *Excelling in Baseball*. San Diego, CA: ReferencePoint Press, 2020.

Bo Mitchell, *Quick Guide to Fantasy Baseball*. San Diego, CA: BrightPoint Press, 2021.

INTERNET SOURCES

Buster Olney, "World Series; In Final Twist, New York Falls in Ninth," *New York Times*, November 5, 2001. www.nytimes.com.

Steve Rushin, "A Series to Savor," *Sports Illustrated*, November 4, 1991. www.vault.si.com.

Tom Verducci, "Game Changer: How Carlton Fisk's Home Run Altered Baseball and TV," *Sports Illustrated*, October 21, 2015. https://si.com/mlb.

WEBSITES

Baseball Reference
www.baseball-reference.com

Baseball Reference is a research website that offers accurate statistical data for every game and player ever associated with Major League Baseball.

Major League Baseball
www.mlb.com

MLB.com is the official website of Major League Baseball and all thirty of its franchises.

Society for American Baseball Research
www.sabr.org

SABR.org is the official website of a membership organization dedicated to preserving the history of baseball.

INDEX

Anderson, Sparky, 10, 17
Armbrister, Ed, 14

Bell, Jay, 44
Brenly, Bob, 40–41, 43
Brosius, Scott, 40
Bryant, Kris, 8, 50, 57

Carbo, Bernie, 17–18
Chapman, Aroldis, 52, 54
Clemens, Roger, 34, 42

Davis, Chili, 27–28
Davis, Rajai, 53, 56

Eastwick, Rawly, 17–18
Evans, Dwight, 13

Fisk, Carlton, 14, 18–21
Fowler, Dexter, 52

Gerónimo, César, 14–15
Gladden, Dan, 32
Gonzalez, Luis, 44–45
Griffey, Ken, 13
Guyer, Brandon, 53, 56

Harper, Brian, 30
Heyward, Jason, 54
Hrbek, Kent, 30–31

Jeter, Derek, 40, 44
Johnson, Randy, 36–37, 41, 43

Kim, Byung-Hyun, 38, 40–41
Kluber, Corey, 48

Larkin, Gene, 32
Leius, Scott, 24
Lemke, Mark, 31
Lynn, Fred, 12, 16–17

Martinez, Michael, 57
Martinez, Tino, 38, 42
Montgomery, Mike, 56
Morgan, Joe, 12, 15, 20
Morris, Jack, 24, 28–33

Napoli, Mike, 48

Peña, Alejandro, 32
Pérez, Tony, 20
Puckett, Kirby, 26, 28

Rivera, Mariano, 35, 43–44
Rizzo, Anthony, 8, 51, 57
Rose, Pete, 18, 20
Russell, Addison, 51

Schilling, Curt, 36–37, 42
Schwarber, Kyle, 7
Smoltz, John, 29, 31
Soriano, Alfonso, 42

Tiant, Louis, 13

Yastrzemski, Carl, 20

Zobrist, Ben, 8

IMAGE CREDITS

Cover: © Ian Johnson/Icon Sportswire/AP Images
5: © Patrick Shemansky/AP Images
7: © Frank Jansky/Icon Sportswire/AP Images
9: © David J. Phillip/AP Images
11: © David Durochik/AP Images
15: © Stan Denny/AP Images
17: © AP Images
19: © Harry Cabluck/AP Images
21: © AP Images
23: © Bill Waugh/AP Images
25: © Jim Mone/AP Images
27: © Jim Mone/AP Images
29: © Jim Mone/AP Images
33: © Mark Duncan/AP Images
35: © David J. Phillip/AP Images
39: © Scott Martin/AP Images
41: © Bill Kostroun/AP Images
43: © Elaine Thompson/AP Images
45: © Matt York/AP Images
47: © Kent Weakley/Shutterstock Images
49: © Frank Jansky/Icon Sportswire/AP Images
51: © Ian Johnson/Icon Sportswire/AP Images
53: © Frank Jansky/Icon Sportswire/AP Images
55: © Paul Beaty/AP Images

ABOUT THE AUTHOR

Ethan Olson is a sportswriter and editor based in Minneapolis, Minnesota.